Flower Making
for Beginners

Also by Priscilla Lobley:

FLOWER MAKING

Flower Making
for Beginners

by PRISCILLA LOBLEY

Taplinger Publishing Company :: New York

First published in the United States in 1971 by
TAPLINGER PUBLISHING CO., INC.
New York, New York

Copyright © 1970 by Priscilla Lobley
All rights reserved. Printed in the U.S.A.

Library of Congress Catalog Card Number: 71-127407

ISBN 0-8008-2805-4

Designed by Lynn Braswell

CONTENTS

PHOTOGRAPHS

INTRODUCTION

Many people seem to think for some reason that flowers are difficult to make. Forget all this. No doubt the professional flower makers have plenty of trade secrets and complicated tools for making their fabulous creations in velvet, voile and muslin. Theirs is, sadly, a dying trade, for flowers are no longer needed to decorate ladies' hats and dresses.

In any case this kind are beyond our scope, and nowadays we make flowers for other purposes: an extravagant dash of color at home perhaps, or as decoration for a party or special occasion.

As a simple and interesting hobby, flower making can teach you a lot about flowers you never noticed before: the way they are constructed and formed; how many petals each variety of flower has; what the stamens really look like and where the calyx grows.

Once you have learned some basic rules and found out where and what materials to buy, you will soon become an enthusiastic flower maker. It may need some perseverance, but remember that paper and wire are not too expensive to buy and so you can afford a few mistakes.

Your skill will certainly impress your friends and you will find giving presents both fun and creative. You will also have the fun of making something that is rather special, and yet costs very little in actual cash.

More than anything else you will need some time and patience. When you are making anything with the skill of your hands, you should not expect immediate results.

I have tried to make the instructions for the flowers as easy to follow as possible, but remember that the flower you make first will always be the slowest to do and the most difficult. By the time you have made a dozen it will be easy!

::1::

ALL YOU NEED

Let's divide the materials we need into four main categories:

1. *Wire.* A basic necessity because you can bend and shape it as you like. You will need three kinds: thick for stems; thin for making leaves and large petals; very fine for fixing petals onto stem.

2. *Paper or Fabric.* To make petals, stamens and leaves, and to cover stems.

3. *String and Other Items.* For making stamens (you can buy nice manufactured ones!).

4. *Tools and Equipment.* Scissors for cutting paper. Pliers for cutting wire. Glue, and cellulose wadding (available from surgical supply stores), for thickening stems or making flower centers. Pins. Plastic tape for binding stems.

Flower making materials are an amalgamation of those used by the florist and millinery trades. Theatrical property departments use some of them as well. You should use your ingenuity to seize on any likely everyday materials that will be useful to you.

WIRE

Florists believe that the wires they use are the tools of their trade, and they therefore, quite understandably, may be reluctant to sell you any. If somebody you know belongs to a flower arranging club you will easily be able to obtain some from this source.

If you cannot come by any florist's wire, don't despair. There is nothing at all special about it. It is simply soft iron wire that is conveniently cut into short lengths and is nice and pliable to use.

You can buy something just as good from any hardware store and it is called galvanized wire. It has the advantage that you can buy it in greater thicknesses than the florist's wire. Real flowers don't need the support that a large handmade sunflower will! The only drawback with it is that you buy it in coils weighing a pound, so you have to straighten it and cut it to the length you require before you can use it.

Wire is often sold by weight. The thickness of it, which is called its gauge, is numbered and, like knitting needles, the thick has low numbers and the thin has high numbers.

A really thick wire for the main stem of large flowers like poppies, lilies or sunflowers would be Nos. 14 or 16.

An average wire for smaller flower stems would be Nos. 16 or 18.

A really thin wire for petals and leaves would be No. 20.

Another very useful wire used by flower makers is cotton-covered wire. It is rather fine, 20 to 30 gauge, and comes in green and white. The same difficulties for buying it may arise as for soft iron wire. Fortunately, the same wire is used for making hats and you should therefore be able to buy it in small white coils from the notions or sewing department of large stores. It will be called millinery wire.

The final type of wire is very, very fine, like fuse wire, and florists call it reel wire. It is best bought on wooden spools, which make it easier to wind it really tight. Hardware stores sell the same wire on small cards and call it floral wire.

PAPER

The most useful stuff by far for flower making is crepe paper. You can easily stretch it to any shape you like, and there is a large selection of colors from which to choose. Dennison's makes about 28 colors and there are two different kinds. You will find that the expensive one stretches much more and has a smoother texture. However, the cheaper brands are quite as good for making most flowers if you can find the colors you want.

Tissue paper also makes pretty flowers but is more limited in what you can do with it. The range of colors is marvelous. You can buy up to 50 different colors. Tissue flowers have a shorter life than crepe ones because the paper has a slight tendency to fade and dull after six months, but I should still use it in spite of this. It is so gorgeous!

Other papers you can use are cellophane, aluminum foil, and gift wrappings. Experiment with anything else that looks interesting and decorative, even cloth and wool yarn.

STRING, ETC.

You don't need to buy much for your flower centers. Most of the time you will probably use fringed paper or string. The manufactured variety of stamens are probably closer to nature than anything one can make, so it's nice to have some of them too.

Buy very coarse sisal string that you can unravel and straighten fairly easily. You will be surprised how effective this looks in the middle of many flowers. You can also have some sealing wax handy to fix on the ends.

TOOLS AND EQUIPMENT

A good sharp pair of scissors that are nicely pointed. (Surgical scissors from the drugstore are ideal.) (See Fig. 1.)

Fig. 1

A pair of pliers for cutting and bending your wire. Woolworth's has a good one in two sizes. (See Fig. 2.)

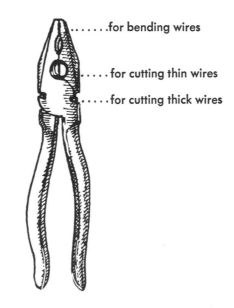

......for bending wires

.....for cutting thin wires

.....for cutting thick wires

Fig. 2

Also have some glue and for this I advise a P.V.A. glue (Polyvinyl Acetate emulsion). You can buy it at stationers or hardware shops. This glue is extremely strong, dries quickly and won't make the wire rusty. To coat a wire with glue, take a small piece of rag and put about a teaspoonful of glue on it. Draw the wire through, taking off surplus with pressure from fingers.

Cellulose wadding is useful for thickening stems, making centers, and even molding fruit. You buy it from the drugstore by the roll and it looks a bit like coarse cotton batting. In the following chapter you will learn how to handle it.

Have on hand a pencil (well-sharpened), pins (the smallest you can find) and, if you are lucky, some special florist's binding tape, which is quite expensive to buy but will last a long time. A florist or flower-arranging club can supply it.

I have now mentioned all the things you may need for making flowers, and perhaps you have a few of them already. Don't rush out and buy them all at once. Acquire them gradually, as you need them. You can start if you like by making a single flower with one piece of paper and wire.

For more help there is a list of special materials and suppliers at the end of the book.

: : 2 : :

TECHNIQUES TO LEARN

There are twenty basic skills that you will find useful to learn and practice. In this chapter each of them is described in detail, with an illustration in most cases.

You may either like to learn these techniques here and now, or you can use this chapter for reference when you need to. I would definitely suggest you try Nos. 1, 2, 3, 4 and 8 because they are fundamental to any flower you may want to make.

They also need a certain amount of practice before you can do them easily, so it is a good idea to master any difficulties before you embark on your first flower. Covering a wire with a narrow strip of crepe paper (No. 4) particularly needs working at before you can do it quickly and perfectly. It is fun to do, however, and worth the effort.

Finally, there are a few facts you need to know about crepe paper. It is a long piece of stuff, usually 20 inches wide and 8½ to 10 feet long. It is rolled round and round into what is called a fold. Thick double paper is two thin layers stuck together and is therefore exactly half the size. The paper only stretches one way which is along the length. The grain (or small lines) run along the width.

With very few exceptions the petals and leaves have the stretch going across and the grain running downward (Fig. 3).

Fig. 3

The instructions are given in working order.

1. CUTTING CREPE PAPER INTO STRIPS

For most stem binding, a strip from ½ inch to 1 inch is the most useful.

Slip the paper out of its wrapper a little way and cut off a strip with good sharp scissors parallel to the wrapper's edge. Keep the fold of paper firmly in your hand while cutting it (Fig. 4).

Fig. 4

In order to cut petals easily, cut your fold in half so you have two strips each 10 inches wide.

N.B.—Always cut your crepe paper this way to ensure the stretch goes in the right direction ACROSS THE GRAIN.

2. FOLDING CREPE PAPER

Take your fold of crepe,which you have cut in half.

Let it unwind completely. Then, taking the two ends together, fold in half. Then fold again . . . and once more to make eight thicknesses of paper (or fold just twice for four thicknesses of double crepe).

Pin each corner to keep secure. You can now easily cut from the paper whenever you like.

3. CUTTING PETALS, ETC., FROM PAPER

Make your patterns on thin cardboard. Draw around them lightly with a pencil or marker.

Draw them as close together as you like, but keep them all going parallel. Pin the center of each with a small pin.

Cut out with scissors, slightly on the inside of your drawing. (Fig. 5.)

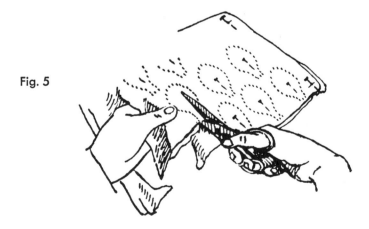

Fig. 5

4. COVERING WIRE WITH NARROW CREPE PAPER STRIP

First put a dab of glue at the top of the wire (or around the base of flower and calyx).

Wrap the binding around and around two or three times very tightly.

Holding the paper in the thumb and forefinger of either your left or right hand, whichever you prefer, twirl the wire around and around with the other hand.

Guide the binding diagonally down, stretching the paper to make it tight. (Fig. 6.)

Fig. 6

When you reach the bottom, break off the paper, dab with glue, and press down.

5. WAYS OF CUTTING FRINGES

Cut a strip of crepe paper as described in Technique No. 1 ACROSS THE GRAIN. It should be the width you want your fringe to be plus about an inch.

Fold into eight and pin here and there to keep paper together.

CUT WITH THE GRAIN as close together as you wish but always leaving at least ½ inch at opposite edge uncut.

You can leave the edges square (see Fig. 7a), or you can cut them in points (see Fig. 7b).

To make a good fringe for centers, fold strip loosely in half down its length. Then fold it up into eight.

Cut close together about ½ inch deep along folded edge. (Fig. 7c.)

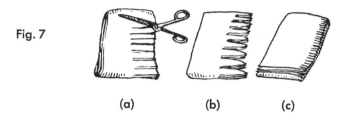

Fig. 7

(a)   (b)   (c)

6. BENDING A WIRE OVER AT TOP TO PREVENT
     CENTER AND PETALS FALLING OFF

Take the top of the wire between thumb and forefinger, turn it over ¼ inch and press together as close as possible.

If you like you can do this with your pliers. (Fig. 8.)

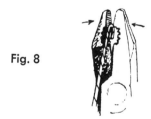

Fig. 8

7. WIRING STRING ONTO STEM

Cut your string an appropriate length to the stamens of the flower you are making. Unravel it and straighten out the kinks. The strands should all be separate.

Having bent over top of wire, lay it against base of string.

Put the thin reel wire against the string at right angles, then wind it around a few times and hook the end over (Fig. 9).

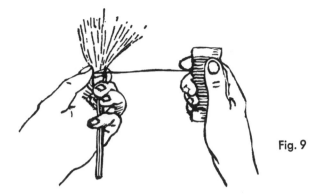

Fig. 9

Continue winding around and around.

Finish off by wrapping reel wire an inch or two down stem before breaking off.

8. WIRING PETALS ONTO STEM

This can sometimes be a tricky business. It is not always easy to get each petal placed where you want it with the wiring holding everything firmly together. Here are some tips.

Have your petals laid out beside you in their correct order.

Hook your reel wire over, as in Technique No. 7, to keep it from slipping.

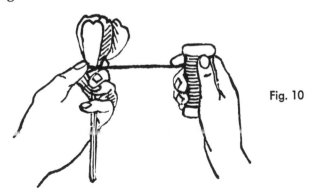

Fig. 10

Overlap your first petals more than you think you should (Fig. 10).

When wiring is finished, dab base of flower with glue if necessary. That will really hold it.

9.   WIRING PETALS DOWN CENTER

If possible use cotton-covered wire. If you have none, you will need very fine wire (20–22 gauge) covered in ¼–inch crepe binding.

Method A

Unpin your petals but keep them together in their groups.

Lift top layer of petals, place glued wire down center of pile as far down to tip as possible. Replace top layer, keeping the two edges exactly together.

Press together and lift off wired petal (Fig. 11a), continue down pile of cut-outs.

If you wish to wire a single layer of paper, proceed as follows.

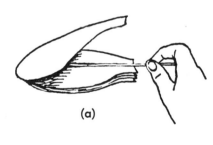

Fig. 11   (a)

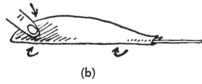

(b)

Method B

Glue wire. Lay on center of petal and double paper over wire (see Fig. 11b). Press down and run thumbnail along inner edge of wire to form center vein. When glue is quite dry, open and press flat.

10. BINDING LEAVES ONTO STEMS

Leaves are not usually glued or wired onto a stem. They are bound in with the crepe paper binding.

Bind down stem in the usual way until you reach the point where the leaf should be.

Place the leaf vertically against the stem (see Fig. 12).

Wind binding two or three times around leaf base and stem. Pull it around as tight as possible.

Continue on down stem.

Fig. 12

11. CUPPING PETALS TO GIVE FLOWERS SOME SHAPE

Place your thumbs in front and fingers outside your petal. Stretch paper across, gently pressing your thumbs inwards to produce a smooth cupped shape at base of petal (see Fig. 13).

Fig. 13

12. FRILLING PETALS

Frill the edges of your petals by scraping edge between the nails of your thumb and forefinger (see Fig. 14).

Fig. 14

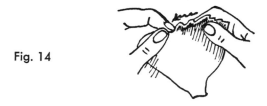

13. CURLING PETALS WITH SCISSORS

Using the inside of your scissors blade and holding petal with one hand, gently scrape the underside of petal. Use the thumb

which is on the scissors to guide the paper across (See Fig. 15).
Simple. Your petal edges are now curled.

Fig. 15

14.   CURLING PETALS WITH A KNITTING NEEDLE OR ORANGE STICK

Place needle at a slant on edge of petal. Wrap paper tightly around (see Fig. 16a) and pull needle out.

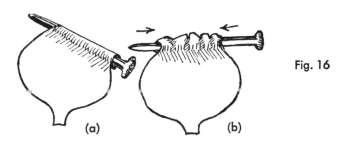

Fig. 16

(a)   (b)

You can, if you want a crinkled effect, push and bunch the paper together, before you remove the needle (see Fig. 16b).

15. CUTTING SERRATIONS FOR LEAVES

Cut your leaves in groups of four or eight, depending on thickness of paper.

Leave the pins in.

Working from the top of the leaf, start making your cuts down the right-hand side (reverse if you are left-handed).

Use your scissors in a curving movement inwards and then bring sharply out again (see Fig. 17).

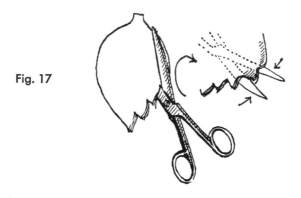

Fig. 17

Hold layers of paper well together in your left hand as close to the edges as you can.

Make your serrations down to the bottom of the leaf.

Turn over and work down the other side from the top again.

16. CUTTING STRIPS OF CELLULOSE WADDING

In order to use cellulose wadding you must make it into strips like crepe binding. Exactly the same rules about stretch apply as in Technique No. 1.

It is advisable to tear it off with your fingers rather than cut it with scissors so you get a good smooth finish when binding with it.

Break about 1½ feet off your roll.

Roll it up again loosely.

Break into strips (Fig. 18).

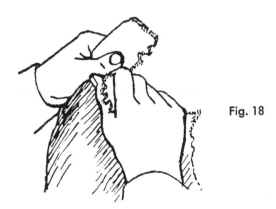

Fig. 18

17.   THICKENING STEMS WITH CELLULOSE WADDING

You can bind a wire with this material to thicken it before you cover stem with crepe paper.

You use it in exactly the same way as Technique No. 4. But as it breaks very easily, you must wrap it around stem wire very gently (Fig. 19).

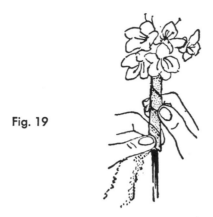

Fig. 19

18.   LENGTHENING STEMS

You can make a stem very much longer if you add several wires in as you are covering it with crepe paper.

Add your first wire about half-way down and double crepe paper binding over to make it stronger.

Add a further two or three wires a little lower down still (Fig. 20).

Make sure top of wires are well-covered with binding, otherwise they will pop out.

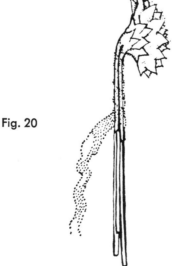

Fig. 20

19.   MAKING VEIN INDENTATIONS

Tear off a square piece of cellulose wadding and lay it on the table.

Put your leaf on top and carefully mark the veins with the scissors blade (see Fig. 21).

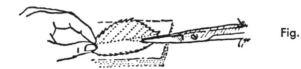

Fig. 21

20.   COLORING AND MARKING CREPE PAPER WITH OIL PASTELS

This is the simplest way, because it does not involve paints and brushes.

You need a small box of oil pastels.

With them you can quickly mark on spots for lilies, poppies, etc.

You may also rub it in to achieve some subtle color changes in your paper.

:: 3 ::

BASIC WAYS OF PUTTING PETALS TOGETHER

1. JOINING ROWS OF PETALS

The easiest way to make a flower is to cut a long strip of paper. Down one side cut fringe or petal shapes. Down the other side bunch paper together. Wrap around and around the stem wire. Wire together at base.

You can use this method to make many varieties of flowers: all kinds of daisies, roses, cherry blossoms, chrysanthemums and sunflowers. (See Fig. 22.)

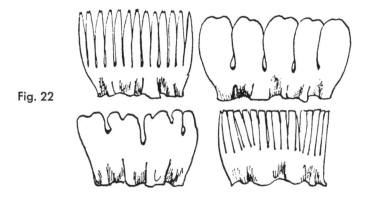

Fig. 22

You can have just one row (Fig. 23) or two or more rows (Fig. 24) or make a pompon effect (Fig. 25).

It is usually better to shape your petals first before you bunch the paper up. Round-shaped petals can be frilled and cupped or even curled with your scissors.

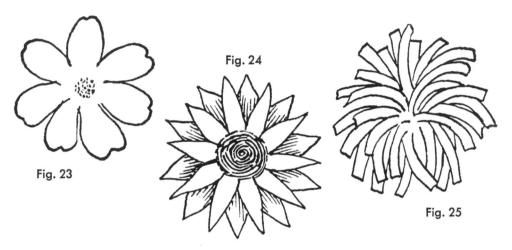

Fig. 24

Fig. 23

Fig. 25

If you are making fringes up into daisies or pompons, it is easier to shape them after you have made them up by gently scraping the paper with the blade of your scissors.

2. CIRCLES OF PETALS IN LAYERS

This method is not very suitable for crepe paper since you will find the grain of the paper going the wrong way on half of your flower.

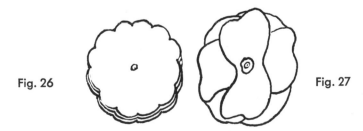

Fig. 26

Fig. 27

It is, however, extremely useful for tissue, cellophane or metallic paper and is also simple to do. You cut your petals out in complete circles (or sections of circles). (See Figs. 26 and 27.)

You can have as many layers as you like. Put stem wire right through center of flower (see Chapter 2, Technique No. 6) and secure with wire or glue. Another good way to secure tissue paper is described in Technique No. 8.

3. WIRE DRAWN OVER CENTER OF PETALS

By this method you can quite quickly make large flowers that are securely and unobtrusively fixed together.

This means of wiring gives a nice, natural, cupped look to the flower.

You can easily work in your stamens as well.

You can either have the petals all going in one direction (see Fig. 28), or you can have them alternating at right angles (see Fig. 29).

Fig. 28 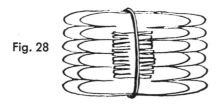  Fig. 29

Then pull your wire really tight and twist the two ends together at the base of the flower.

If possible, use some cotton-covered wire to do this so that, if it does show a little, it won't be too noticeable.

Shape your petals before you lay them down to wire up. Also bunch the paper together in the center.

Plate 5 shows the flowers when finished.

4.   MADE UP FROM REAL FLOWERS

Following this method you literally take a real flower and cut your petals and sepals in paper to exactly the same shape using the real flower parts as a pattern.

Wiring them if necessary, you fix them together in exactly the same order as your real flower.

This method is explained fully in the next chapter.

:: 4 ::

COPYING REAL FLOWERS

You can't go wrong if you make some flowers from close observation of real ones. Although you can have a lot of fun doing clever things with paper, the knowledge and pleasure that come from copying flowers will give you something lasting.

It will make you look at a flower more closely than you ever have before. You will have to know for sure exactly the shape, number and position of the petals. What is more, you will not forget what you learn. You might even find yourself improving at botany and plant drawing, for you will certainly be expanding your knowledge of flowers.

In this chapter you will find out how to set about copying real flowers from start to finish. Exactly the same method can be used to copy any flower you like, from the most simple wild flower to the most elaborate orchid.

Choose a medium-sized flower for your first effort, such as an anemone, single rose, clematis or poppy.

Have two similar flowers, one to pull apart and one to copy.
Have your materials ready:

    Wire, medium thickness, 16 or 18 gauge.

    Thick or thin crepe paper for petals and calyx.

    Thin crepe paper for binding stems.

    String for center.

(It is only possible to reproduce a flower with complete accuracy if you make it up in white paper and then paint it yourself, copying every detail from subtle color changes to various patterns and markings. This is difficult to start with and can take quite a long time. So I suggest you begin by making your flowers in the nearest shade of paper you can buy.)

Look at the diagram (Fig. 30) and learn the names for the various parts of the flower.

Fig. 30

Pistil { Stigma / Style / Ovary

Anther } Stamen
Filament

Calyx (sepals)

First carefully remove the calyx (sepals) and flatten them out in one piece (Fig. 31). Put them safely to one side.

Fig. 31

Next gently remove the petals one-by-one and note if there are any variations in size. If they are all the same size just keep one.

If there are two or more different shapes and sizes keep one of each.

Now, find a piece of thin cardboard from an old cereal carton or box, and sharpen a pencil.

Lay the calyx flat downwards on the cardboard and, holding firm with thumb and forefinger, draw round the edges with your pencil. Do exactly the same with the petals (see Fig. 32).

Add a bit extra to the base of them both to enable you to fix them on the stem (Fig. 33).

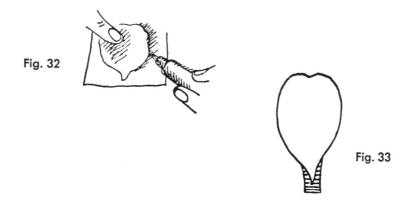

Fig. 32

Fig. 33

Next, cut your patterns out from the cardboard very carefully with scissors and write on the pieces the name of the flower they come from. Also find an envelope and label that too so that you have somewhere safe to keep your patterns when you have finished making the flower. You may want to make them again later on when the flowers are not in bloom.

Lastly, look at your flower center and see what is going on there. Do not be ambitious at first. In most cases a small chunk of natural-colored sisal string for tying up parcels will answer the purpose.

Now cut your petals and calyx out in paper. If you have been able to buy the thick double crepe paper, this will be the easier for your first attempt. If not, the thin crepe always looks nice and delicate.

Take your fold of paper, and if it is 20 inches wide cut it in half. Fold it into eight layers (or four if it is double crepe). Secure each corner with a pin. See Technique Nos. 1 and 2 in Chapter 2. Now put your patterns down and draw lightly around them the correct number of petals you will need. You can draw them as close as you like for economy but the grain or stretch of the paper must go across them (see Technique No. 3).

Pin through the middle of each drawing to hold the pieces of paper together and then cut out with your scissors, slightly on the inside of your pencil line.

1. If you are making anemones you should have approximately ten petals looking like Fig. 34.

Fig. 34

2. If you are making a wild poppy there are four petals (Fig. 35).

3. The single rose has five petals and calyx (Fig. 36).

Fig. 35   Fig. 36

Take your wires, which should be about 7–10 inches long. Cover them in thin crepe paper which you have cut into ½-inch wide strips. (See Chapter 2, Technique No. 4.) Use a green paper with a fairly subtle color.

You will probably need a fair amount of practice before your stem binding is really tight and smooth. It will come with perseverance. Don't forget that a dab of glue at the top and bottom helps to keep the binding in place.

Cover all your wires with paper, which you must always do unless you are using cotton-covered wire. Next turn the top over ¼ inch to prevent the petals and string falling off! You can use your pliers if you like to squeeze it close together.

Cut a bunch of string about the same size as the stamens of your flower. Make it straight and fix it on to your stem wire with fine reel wire.

If you are making an anemone, paint the string with black ink or paint and allow to dry.

Do make absolutely sure that all your string is wired tightly and securely. Next wire around your petals in the same way. Do this one at a time and keep your wire extremely tight. Fix them so that they are as nearly as possible in the same position as the petals on your real flower.

When you have fixed your petals in place, go on winding your wire around and around your stem to secure it before you cut it off. The next step is to glue the base of the calyx and wrap it around the base of the flower, holding it in place until it is firmly stuck. Then bind over it and down your wire with a finishing layer of crepe paper, gluing it down at the bottom.

All you have to do finally is to give the different parts of the flower some shape. Have another good look at the real one. Separate the strands of string to look like stamens and trim with scissors if necessary (Fig. 37). Frill the edges of your petals and cup them. (See Chapter 2, Technique Nos. 11 and 12.) If you are making a rose, roll the edges over an orange stick or knitting needle (Technique No. 14).

Push some shape into the calyx and curve the wire of the stem.

Of course, you can elaborate this basic method in many ways. If you want to make a larger flower, like a lily, you can wire two layers of paper together to make bigger and stronger petals.

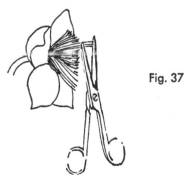

Fig. 37

Alternatively, you can stick shapes of petals together to form a trumpet-shaped flower, like a rhododendron or morning glory.

You can also make fantastic features of pistil and stamens, as in gladioli and hibiscus.

The point is that you can turn paper and wire into practically any shape you like. No flower is impossible to copy in this way, as long as you have one right in front of you.

:: 5 ::

HINTS ON FLOWER
CENTERS AND LEAVES

It is hard to say for certain which method is best for making the stamens of flowers. In many cases the manufactured ones are closest to the real thing. A reasonable substitute is string as described in Technique No. 7 (p. 22). This can be improved with some sealing wax on tips, which you should do before you have made the flower up. Modeling paste mixed with a little paint can also be used in the same way, or alternatively you can dab spots of Elmer's Glue-All on top and, when quite dry, cover over with yellow paint.

If you are making flowers more for decoration than realism, then cut, fringed paper looks very pretty. You can dab brown or orange ink on it for some extra interest.

An easy way to make two types of large stamens for flowers of the lily family is to cut some 7-inch lengths of cotton-covered wire, or cover some fine, 20 gauge wire yourself. (a) Bend your wire as in Fig. 38, fill anther with glue and paint when dry. (b) Leave your wire straight and stick on a paper shape as in Fig. 39.

Fig. 38   Fig. 39

Making the pistil is usually just a matter of clever binding. If you want to make a pronounced stigma, you need to double your bind, glue it onto the wire and then go around and around tightly and neatly until it is the required size. Then bind down stem as usual (see Fig. 40).

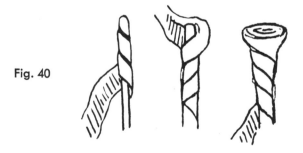

Fig. 40

To make a round seed pod, bind the shape gently with cellulose wadding onto a wire that has been bent over at the top. Cover it over and over as smoothly as possible with ½-inch crepe paper binding and glue down.

Leaves can be just as decorative as flowers and are their natural complement in color. It seems a pity to neglect them. Each variety of plant has leaves of a different shape, size and color. You should always remember to observe the structure of them as closely as you do a flower. It is possible, if you like, to make up leaves as a decoration on their own.

In Chapter 2 you can find out how to serrate edges when you cut them out. If your flowers are for fun, and to make a vivid splash of color, I suggest you choose a gaudy, green-colored paper for the leaves.

Cut them out in larger-than-life shapes and bind them in with abandon.

If you would prefer the leaves to be quieter and closer to nature, then follow the method described in Chapter 4. Use a subtle shade of leaf-green paper and draw on the veins with soft-colored crayons.

Try using two different shades of green if you are making two-layered leaves, wired down the center. Do not forget that leaves need some shaping, as do flowers. Curve the center wire and frill the edges.

When you are mounting them on the main stem, try to achieve the effect of something growing. See how the leaves are spaced and if they grow in pairs.

Put in some offshoots if possible and when you have mounted all your leaves together, curve and bend the main stem.

::6::

TEN FLOWERS TO MAKE

*Step-by-Step Instructions for Making
Tissue Pompons, Azaleas, Daisies, Poppies,
Sweet Peas, Rose- or Lotus-type Flowers,
Lilies, Morning Glory and Giant Flowers*

Easiest ones come first!

TISSUE POMPONS

MATERIALS

The brightest colors of tissue paper you can get. Two sheets make
one big flower. Stem wires, 14 or 16 gauge. Reel wire.

Cut your tissue into 10-inch squares. Flowers can be all the
same color or varied, as you wish.

1 Take 10 or 12 squares

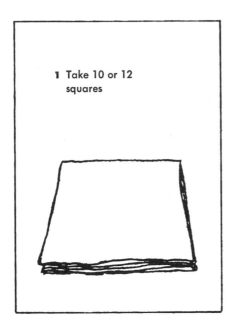

2 Fold in half . . .

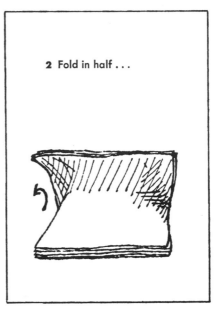

3 and then again . . .

4 . . . and then once again

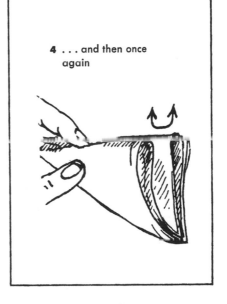

5 Trim petal shape like this.

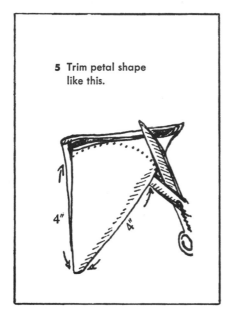

6 Spread out flat.

Make two holes in center with a pin . . .

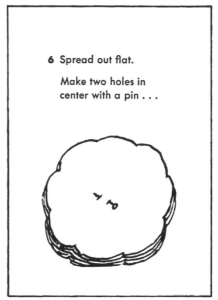

7 . . . and thread a length of reel wire through them.

8 Squeeze together at base to form a funnel shape

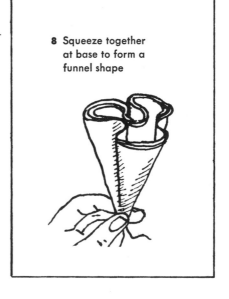

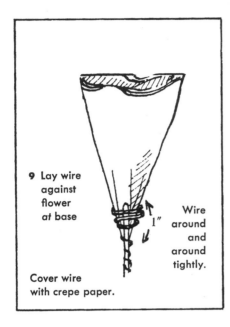

9 Lay wire against flower at base

Wire around and around tightly.

1"

Cover wire with crepe paper.

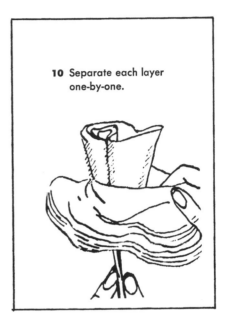

10 Separate each layer one-by-one.

11 Now, holding base of flower firmly, pull and pleat middle petals back up into a vertical position. Separate and ruffle up to look like petals.

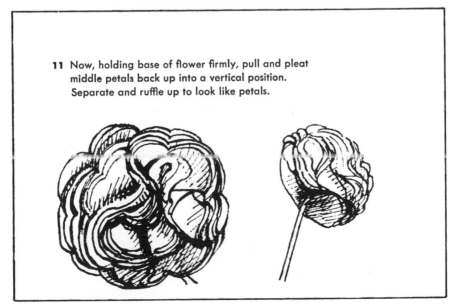

P.S.—If you want a fringed edge cut it at Stage 5.

AZALEAS

MATERIALS

Thin crepe paper. Try out warm pinks, yellows and oranges for flowers. Green for stem covering. Stem wires, 16 or 18 gauge, about 10 inches long. Reel wire.

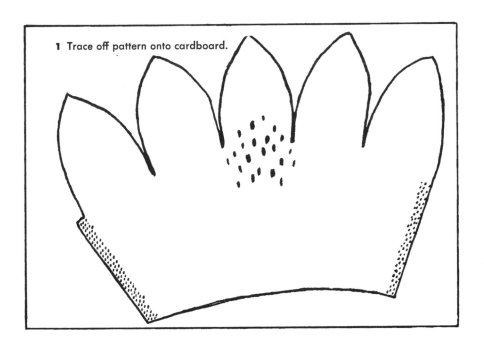

1 Trace off pattern onto cardboard.

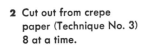

2 Cut out from crepe paper (Technique No. 3) 8 at a time.

3 Draw on pattern with red marker.

4 Cover your stem wires with extremely narrow stem binding in the same color as the flower.

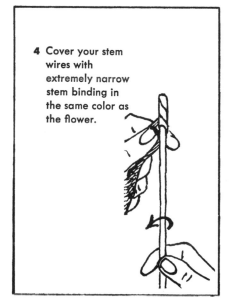

5 Glue shaded edges of flower and stick together.

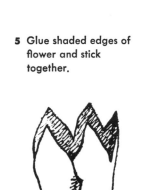

6 Insert a covered stem wire so that top is level with the tips of petals.

7 Wire around base with reel wire.

8 Bind over stem with green paper.

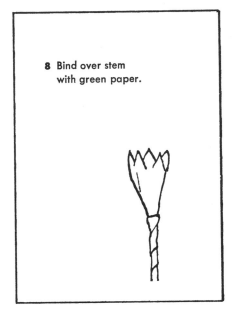

9 Frill petal edges and then cup them.

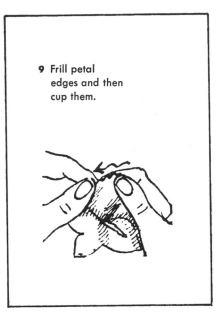

Some flowers from the outside

others from the inside

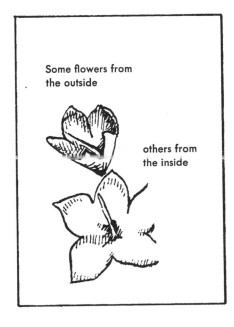

10 Slightly curve center wire.

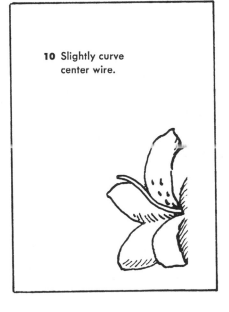

DAISIES

MATERIALS

Thin crepe paper. Any color will probably work, but try mauve or white for petals—yellow for stamens and dark green for center and stems. Stem wires, 16 or 18 gauge and 10 inches long. Reel wire.

1 From your green paper cut off a 1-inch
strip. From this cut an 8-inch length.

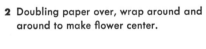

2 Doubling paper over, wrap around and
around to make flower center.

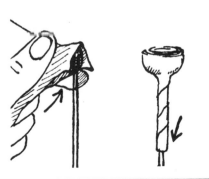

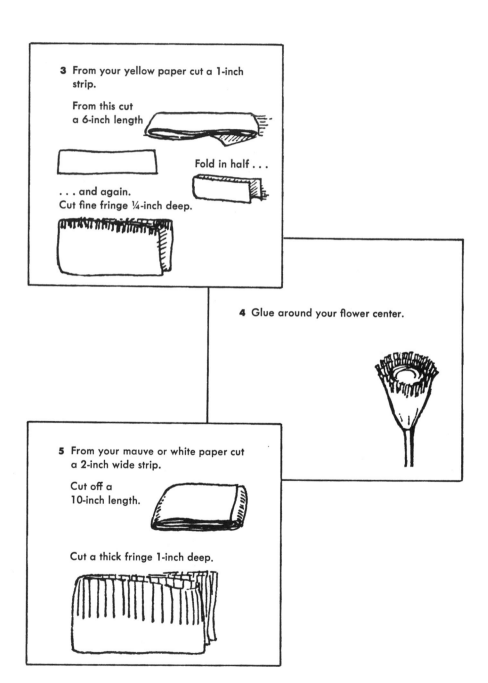

3 From your yellow paper cut a 1-inch strip.

From this cut a 6-inch length

Fold in half . . .

. . . and again. Cut fine fringe ¼-inch deep.

4 Glue around your flower center.

5 From your mauve or white paper cut a 2-inch wide strip.

Cut off a 10-inch length.

Cut a thick fringe 1-inch deep.

6 Wrap around your flower as evenly as possible and wire tightly with reel wire.

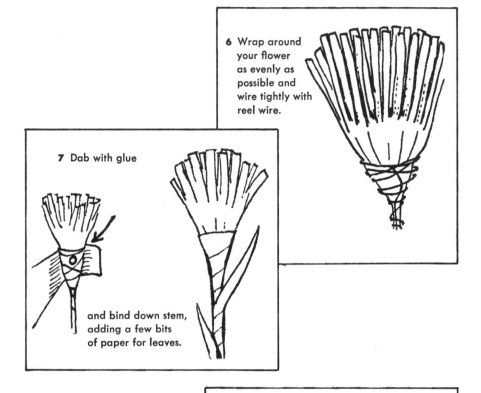

7 Dab with glue

and bind down stem, adding a few bits of paper for leaves.

8 Shape flower by spreading out fringe and GENTLY scraping with scissors.

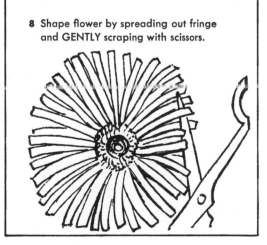

POPPIES

MATERIALS

Thin crepe paper. Any color you like for flowers. Black for center. Grey-green for stem. Stem wires, 14 or 16 gauge, 18 to 24 inches length. Reel wire.

1 Make center of ¾-inch diameter with cotton batting or cellulose wadding. Dab glue on stem wire to prevent it falling off.

2 With ½-inch strip of black paper cover over as smoothly as you can.

3 Cut a strip of black paper 3½ inches wide. Cut off a 12-inch length.

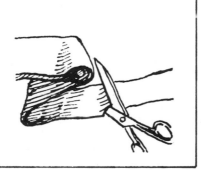

4 Fold down the middle.

5 Join both ends together

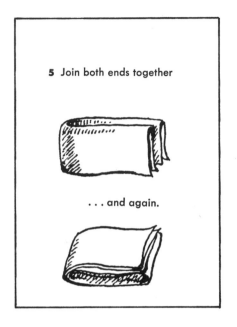

. . . and again.

6 And cut fine fringe about ⅜ inch deep along FOLDED edge.

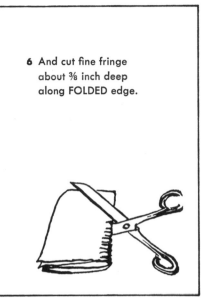

7 Wrap loosely around center and secure tightly with wire.

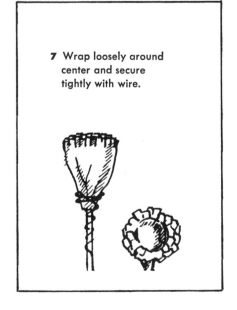

8 Cut a 5-inch wide strip for petals and cut off 6-inch lengths for each petal. (4 petals make a flower.)

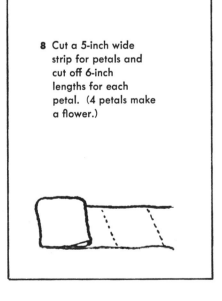

9 Cut off corners in a
curve and bunch paper
up to give a
poppy look.

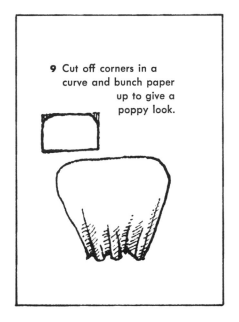

10 Wire on petals in
pairs.

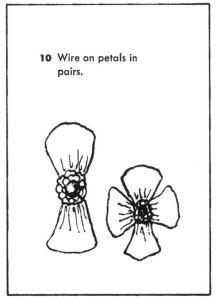

11 Frill petal edges and
slightly cup base of
petals.

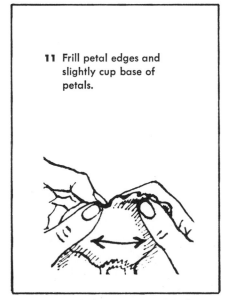

12 Cover stems and
give them some
interesting bends.

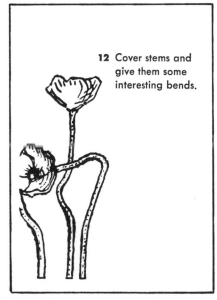

P.S.—Put on black or maroon-colored spots with oil pastels.

SWEET PEAS

MATERIALS

Thin crepe paper. Any amount of color variation: pinks, mauves, scarlet, purple, white, salmon. Green-covered tray wire for flower stems and tendrils. For main stems, 10-inch lengths of 16 or 18 gauge wire and green paper. Make lots and lots of flowers.

1 Trace off patterns onto cardboard.

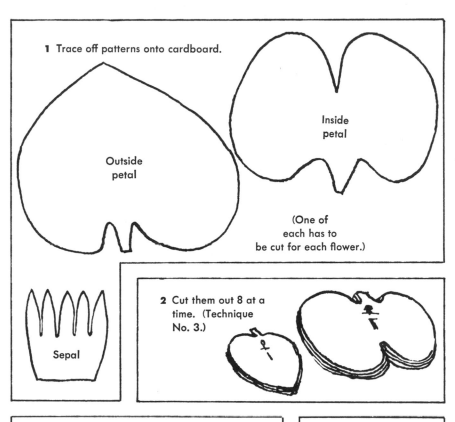

Outside
petal

Inside
petal

(One of
each has to
be cut for each flower.)

Sepal

2 Cut them out 8 at a
time. (Technique
No. 3.)

3 Gently scrape the
edge of each petal
between scissors-
blade and thumb to
make it curl over.

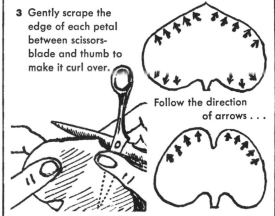

Follow the direction
of arrows . . .

4 . . . to shape petals
like this.

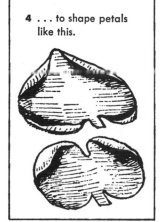

5 With petals curling
INWARDS—dab
with glue as indicated.

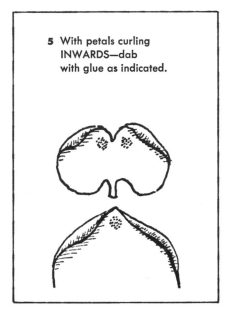

6 Press together here
until glue holds.

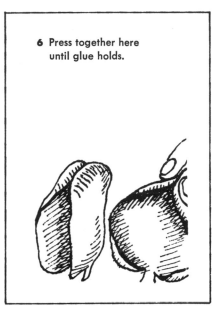

7 Lay down an out-
side petal and dab
on some glue. Then
place on a 4-inch
length of tray wire
bent over at top.

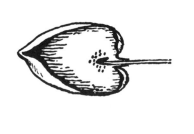

8 Then lay the inside
petal on top and
pinch together at
base of flower till
glue holds.

9 Spread glue on base of sepal and stick around base of flower to make a tight-fitting collar.

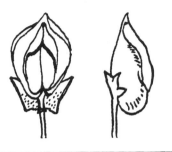

10 Make some tendrils by winding a small length of tray wire

around an orange stick.

11 Bind your flowers in sprays of 2, 3 or 4.

12 Bend flowers over and curve main stems in gentle S-bends.

ROSE- OR LOTUS-TYPE FLOWERS

MATERIALS

Thin crepe paper in any color you like. Cotton-covered tray
wire for wiring petals. Stem wires about 14 gauge. Stem binding.

ROSE

1 Cut paper in half to make a 10-inch wide strip.

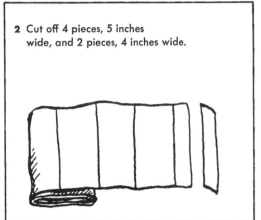

2 Cut off 4 pieces, 5 inches wide, and 2 pieces, 4 inches wide.

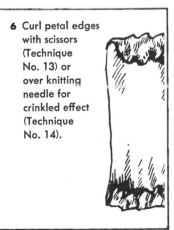

3 Round off edges of 5-inch pieces with scissors.

4 Trim one 4-inch piece like this . . .

5 And fringe the other like this

(to make your stamens).

6 Curl petal edges with scissors (Technique No. 13) or over knitting needle for crinkled effect (Technique No. 14).

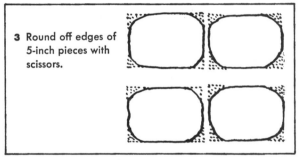

7 Squeeze petals and stamens together in center.

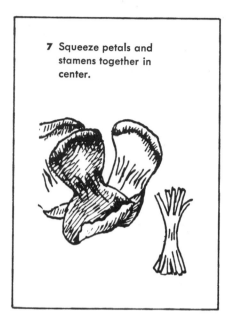

8 Now, starting with large petals, lay them one on top of the other.

in opposite directions.

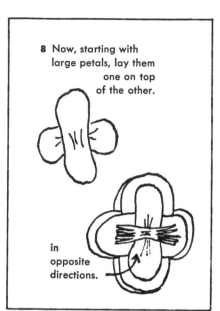

9 Wrap a length of tray wire around center in a cross.

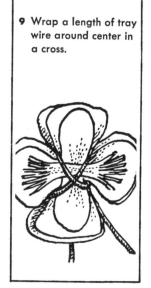

10 Draw up petals together tightly and twist the two ends of wire together at base of flower.

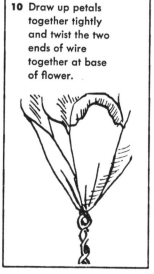

11 Spread petals out, reshape to look like rose. Bind down stem adding another wire.

LOTUS

1 Make petals as for rose, but cut 10 of them 3½ inches wide.

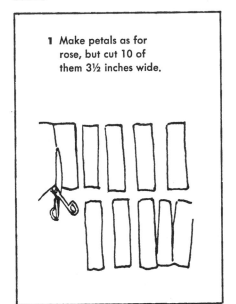

2 Round edges of 9 like this . . .

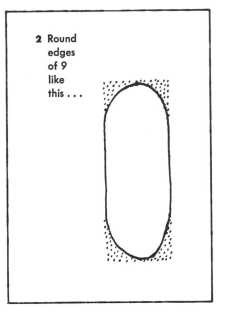

3 . . . and cut one fringed.

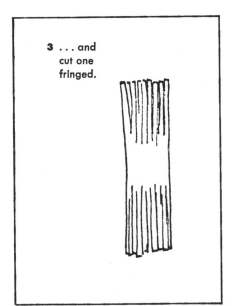

4 Scrape edges so they turn inwards.

Carry on as for rose.

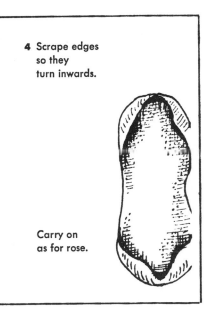

LILIES

This pattern is for a tiger lily. But by varying the size and coloring you can make all sorts of lilies in this way.

MATERIALS

Thin crepe paper. Pale orange for petals and dark orange for stamens. Green for stem binding and leaves. Green and white-covered wire for stamens and petals if possible. For flower stem, wire 18 gauge and 10 inches long. For main stem, 14 gauge and 20 inches long.

1 Trace patterns onto cardboard. Large petal.
Small petal. Each is double-layered.
3 large and 3 small to a flower.

2 Cut plenty of petals
out 8 at a time.
(Technique No. 3.)

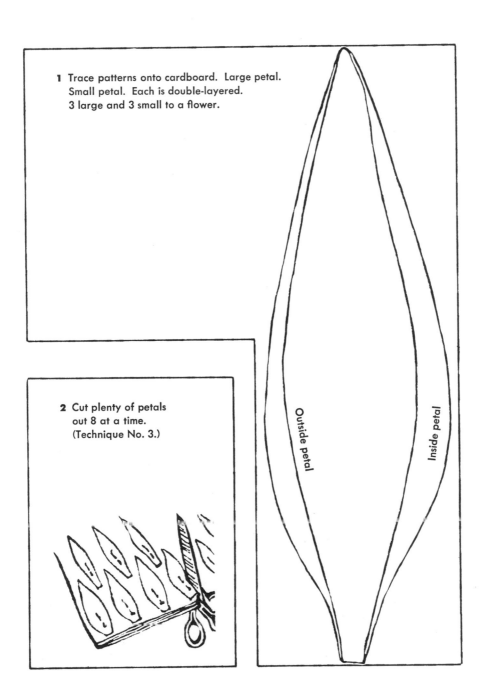

Outside petal

Inside petal

3 Wire petals.
(Technique No. 9a.)

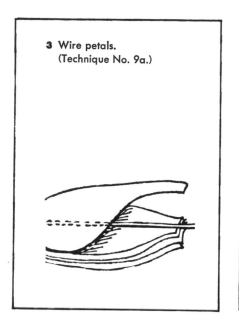

4 Mark on spots with
black marker.

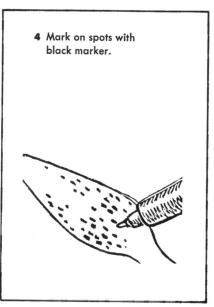

5 Cover and thicken 2½
inches of an 18 gauge
wire to form pistil.

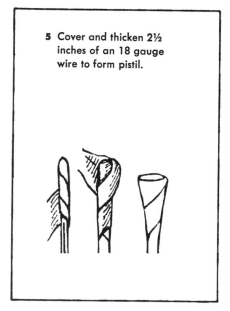

6 Cut out from red
paper shapes for
stamens about 1 inch
long and stick on
to 2½-inch lengths
of green tray
wire.

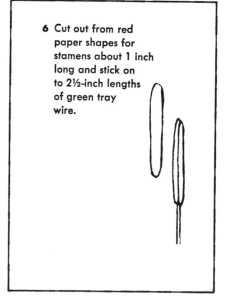

7 Bind six stamens around your stigma with reel wire.

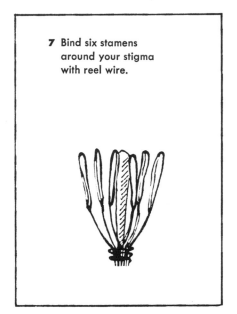

8 ... then wire your petals around.

first the three large petals,

then the three small ones in the gaps.

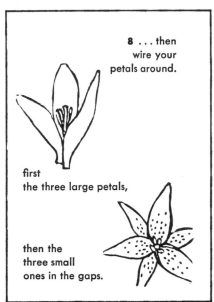

9 Bind down stem and curve the petals into place.

Frill them as well

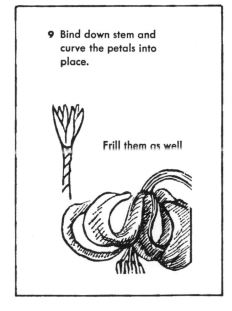

10 Bind flowers onto thicker wire, together with some unwired paper leaves.

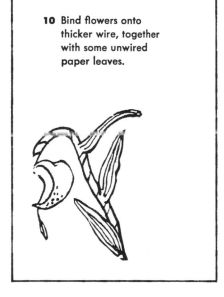

MORNING GLORY

MATERIALS

Thin or thick crepe paper (you will find the thick is the easier to manage), white and pale blue or pink for flowers, pale green for sepals and stems. For stem wires, 16 or 18 gauge and 10 inches long. Reel wire.

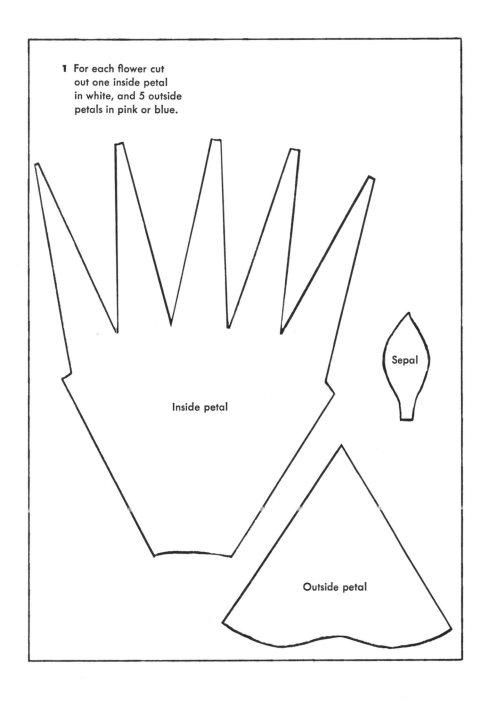

1 For each flower cut
  out one inside petal
  in white, and 5 outside
  petals in pink or blue.

Inside petal

Sepal

Outside petal

2 Glue each outside petal down one side only first. Overlap as little as possible.

3 Then glue down the other side.

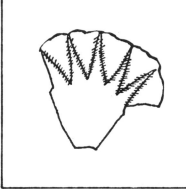

4 Then glue outside edges together.

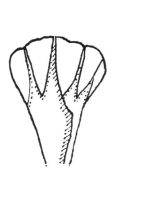

5 Cover a stem wire with white paper and glue a bit of white fringe around the top.

6 Drop wire through center of flower and wire base on to it with reel wire.

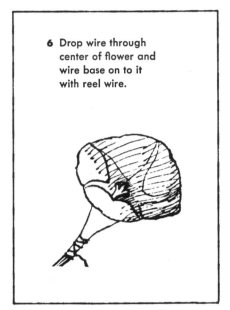

7 Cut 3 sepals for each flower and glue them in place.

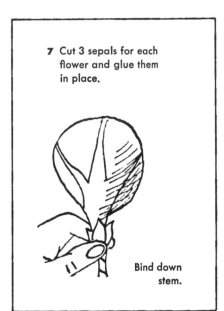

Bind down stem.

8 Put lots of bends and loops in stem to give bindweed effect.

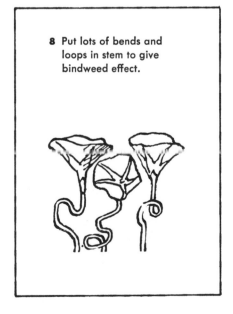

9 Mount onto trailing stems with a few leaves.

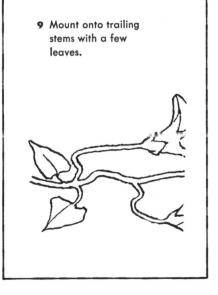

GIANT FLOWERS

This way you can build up a flower to enormous proportions. The ones made here are 12 inches across, but you could add more strips of petals to make them larger if you like. Their stunning effect depends a lot on the colors you make them in. Always use two shades of a color for the petals, and two colors for the center, with the lighter one outside.

There are two different centers described but the patterns for the petals are exactly the same.

ARTICHOKE (the easier flower)

MATERIALS

Thin crepe paper. I've used two shades of cyclamen pink for petals, salmon pink and scarlet for the center. For stem wire use 14 gauge and 24-inch length. You need four for each flower.

1 *To make center—cut* 6-inch strip in both colors.

2 From salmon pink strip cut off 3-foot length

and fold in four.

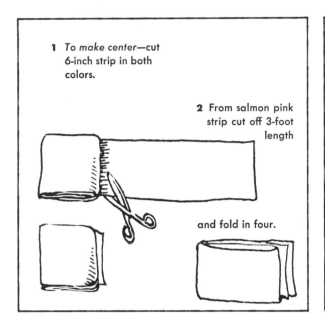

3 Cut pointed ¼-inch fringe 3 inches deep.

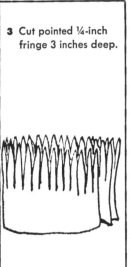

4 Gather and pleat together at base . . .

then wrap around and around one stem wire and secure with reel wire.

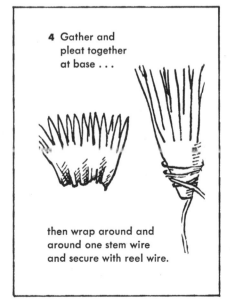

5 From your scarlet strip cut off 4-foot length and cut fringe as before.

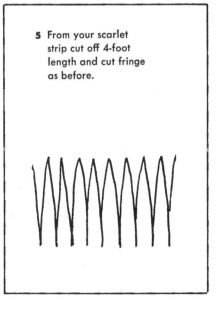

6 Pleat together and wrap around the salmon-pink fringe.

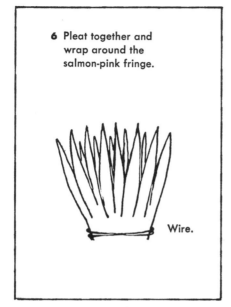

Wire.

7 For *petals*—there are 5 rows. Cut an 8-inch wide strip in darker paper.

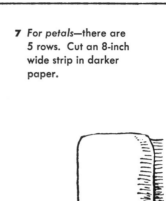

8 1st row. Cut off 13-inch length and trim 1 inch off width.

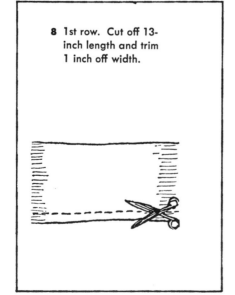

9 Cut 10 petals 3 inches deep . . . just over 1¼ inches wide.

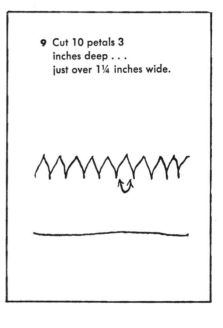

10 Wrap around flower.

Secure with reel wire
1 inch higher than
center fringe.

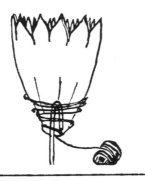

11 2nd row. Cut off
another length 14½
inches long.

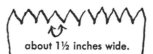

... and
trim off ½ inch.

Cut 10 petals 3 inches deep,

about 1½ inches wide.

12 Bind around on top
of 1st row,
about ½ inch higher.

13 3rd row. Cut another
length 16½ inches
long.
And cut 10 petals.

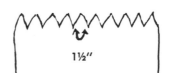

1½"

Bind around as before ...
about ½ inch higher.

14 For final rows in lighter color cut off a 9½-inch strip.

Bind around as before . . . about ½ inch higher.

15 4th row. Cut 22-inch length.

Trim off 1 inch.

16 Cut 10 petals 3 inches deep . . .

about 2¼ inches wide.

17 Bind around exactly as before, and glue two edges together.

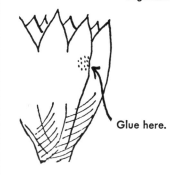

Glue here.

18 Cut off 24-inch length . . .

about 2¼ inches wide.

Cut 11 petals and repeat exactly as before.

19 In brown crepe, cut a strip 7 inches wide and 16 inches long.

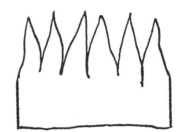

Cut sepals like 1st row petals.

20 Stick around with glue.

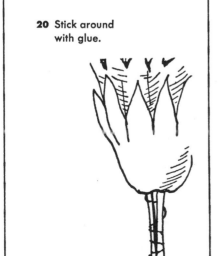

21 Add another 1 or 2 rows and then

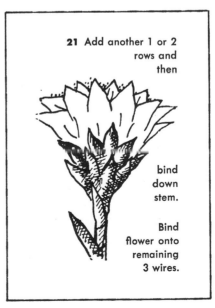

bind down stem.

Bind flower onto remaining 3 wires.

SUNFLOWER

MATERIALS

Thin crepe paper. Two shades of deep bright yellow for petals and brown for center. Stem wires, 14 gauge and 24 inches long.

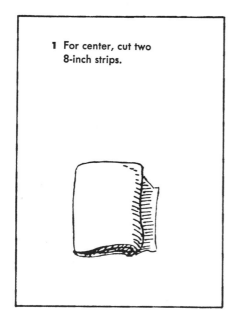

1 For center, cut two 8-inch strips.

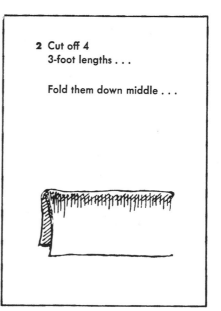

2 Cut off 4 3-foot lengths . . .

Fold them down middle . . .

3 . . . and fold up 3 times.

4 Cut ½-inch-deep fringe down folded edge. (Technique No. 5.)

5 Gather and bunch them together at base.

Wrap around stem wire, wiring fringes on one at a time.

6 Carry on with petals as stages 8-21 artichoke flower.

: : 7 : :

EXTRA IDEAS

You can extend flower making to plenty of other things besides crepe and tissue paper, but because these are so easy to use and can produce attractive and spectacular results I've spent most time with them.

In this chapter I've added a few ideas which you can try out if you like, or they may help you with some ideas of your own.

1. GLASS BEAD SPARKLERS

These don't look realistic but remind one of grasses with frost on them.

You will need cotton-covered tray wire in white, and glass beads. Keep to one color but vary the sizes.

Cut the wire into 18-inch lengths. Poke some glue into center of your bead and thread it into place about 8 or 10 inches down your wire. When it is stuck, do the next one, keeping the gaps about ¾ inch apart. Bind each beaded wire into bunches of seven or nine with white paper binding. (Fig. 41.)

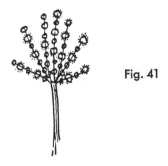

Fig. 41

2. *WOOL FLOWERS*

These were very popular one hundred years ago, and you may still see some examples carefully preserved under glass domes. I don't think nowadays we have the inclination to put so much intricate detail and effort into handwork, but you can easily make some simple flowers by a similar method.

Fig. 42   Fig. 43

You can buy tapestry wool in a wide range of lovely colors, from the most subtle to the most vivid. This is certainly superb to use because you can choose exactly what colors you want for stems and leaves as well as petals. To be economical, at first you can of course raid the wool bag.

You will also need cotton-covered wire.

Make the structure of the petals in your covered wire and fix it into place with reel wire (Fig. 42). Cut your stamens in wool and, if you like, knot pieces in contrasting wool at the ends.

Fill in the petal structure horizontally with wool, fixing it to wire each time with a knot as shown (Fig. 43). Wire your petals around your stamens and cover stem around and around tightly with wool (Fig. 44). Make leaves in the same way, threading some wool down center for veins, and mount them in down stem. Match your wools to the colors of real flowers.

Fig. 44

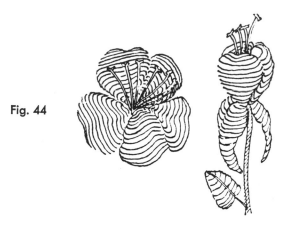

3. RAFFIA ONION SWAGS

Use two colors of raffia—Fawn and brown;
Yellow and gold;
White and fawn;
or
Maroon and brown.

For stem wires, use cotton-covered wire or 16 or 18 gauge wire covered with neutral-colored crepe paper.

Cut some short lengths of raffia in the main color and wire onto main stem. Trim it to look like onion roots (Fig. 45); 2½ inches from roots, wire on onion tops. Next make your onion shape with cellulose wadding strips (Fig. 46) as firmly and tightly as possible. Then wind your main color raffia around and around, using a needle to thread it through in places. Go on until no cellulose wadding shows through.

Finally, with your contrasting color make a striped effect (Fig. 47).

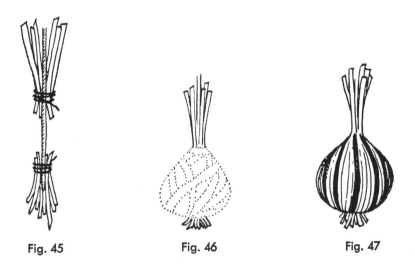

Fig. 45   Fig. 46   Fig. 47

To put onions into a swag, first make about a dozen onions. Knot enough raffia to make a thick plait. Twist it together a few times and then start plaiting in your onion stems. When they are all in, continue plaiting a little more and then finish off with a knot. Fix a loop at the top for hanging swag on wall.

CONCLUSION:
USING YOUR FLOWERS

If you have made some enormous flowers you will probably want to put them on very long stems. Buy some bamboo canes from your hardware store, picking out the smoothest ones. Bind one in with the stem wire, but remember that you won't be able to curve the stem now because cane doesn't bend.

Another type of cane that you may find useful is the sort used in basket-making. It is called center cane. It can be bought in different thicknesses from handicraft shops. It is extremely pliable and must be used with wire. It makes up into very light flexible stems.

When you are putting flowers and leaves together, make the stems as interesting as possible. Add tendrils made with cotton-covered wire, aerial roots cut from string or even paper rose thorns. Color the stems to give some extra interest.

Try putting your flowers into swags or garlands. This is very easy. Simply bind the stems over and over with reel wire, two at a time.

Keeping flowers in place in a vase or container sometimes raises difficulties. Cut a small piece of chicken wire with your pliers, roll it into a loose ball and push it carefully into your vase. Unless this is transparent glass it won't show, and it will certainly prevent the sprays falling about.

Another good thing to use is modeling clay. You can wedge a lump into a jar or flower pot, stick your flower stem into it, and you have a potted plant!

A more permanent way to fix a flower into a pot is to mix some sand and plaster with a little water (you can buy small bags ready-mixed). Pour into a flower pot, which you have lined with newspaper. Then fix stem into mixture as it starts to harden.

If you don't like the look of plaster around your flower stem, cover with some dried moss.

Make sure that your flowers always look as nice as possible. Don't be tempted to stand them right by the window, because the direct light, especially in the summer, will dull the color. It is much better to place them where they will catch some reflected lamp light in the evening.

Finally, be adventurous with the flowers you make. Look around you for inspiration. Books and pictures can be helpful. So can other people's efforts. Smart shop windows and imported paper flowers are well worth looking at.

Place them with nice things like old pieces of china and glass, dried seedpots and grasses, and when they look a little faded—make some more.

SOURCE INDEX

Thick crepe paper, stamens, cotton-covered tray wire, and other flower making sundries may be ordered by mail directly from:

> Priscilla Lobley Flower Kits
> Thorpe Lodge, Ealing Green
> London W.5
> England

Most basic wires may be purchased at hardware stores or florist suppliers.

Crepe papers, tissue papers, glues, raffia, scissors and other small tools and craft suppliers may be purchased at hobby shops, Woolworth stores and at larger stationery and supply stores.

Larger florists carry many finer wires and stem-binding tapes and can also supply cork bark, moss and other materials required for making flowers or finishing arrangements.

Sea fern, coral, shells and other decorative trimmings may usually be purchased at larger aquarium supply shops.

Cellulose wadding may be purchased at large drug stores or from surgical or doctor's supply dealers.